Web Design for Beginners:

The Ultimate Website Beginners Guide for learning Professional website design

Table Of Contents

Introduction

Just like other fields of design, web design is constantly and rapidly evolving. With billions of websites on the internet today, you could be right to compare website developers with bees as far as being busy is concerned. Compare how much web designers had to do to build a website back then, and just how little they have to do today to do the same – what do you see? It is clearly evident that web designers have become smarter with time.

Being a smart web designer, however, is not something that you become overnight. It is a learning process that starts right here! Well, this is an eBook that contains almost everything that a newbie needs to know about web design. If you want to redesign your business or company website or are just interested in building a revenue generating website, you'll find this detailed guide both informative and instructive. Let's get right to it, shall we?

Web Design Facts that are Worth Knowing

To truly comprehend the web design process, it is important that you look past the outward visual appearance of a website. You should consider what actually happens behind the scenes when making a website as that's what determines the kind of experience and/or engagement users will ultimately have with that particular website. The following are the web design facts that you should be well acquainted with prior to developing a website:

1. **Websites look different across different browsers**

Different web browsers render websites differently, which means that the same website you view on your PC using Mozilla Firefox might look completely different when viewed on Google Chrome. This is because web browsers translate code differently, and even vary in the manner in which they translate it on different screens. While one browser may load a code in a very specific order, another may even fail to recognize the same code altogether.

To ensure that your website will provide a great experience to every user regardless of the browser they are using, it's important that you be familiar with CSS and HTML standards. This will help you to create a website that not only looks good but also one that functions properly across various browsers. You should also take your time to perform extensive browser compatibility testing to discover potential issues, and make appropriate fixes for those issues before the website goes live.

2. **There is a difference between mobile design and responsive design**

Most people are often amazed at the seemingly magical conversion that happens when they switch between their computer and smartphone, but not many of them realize that there's a difference between mobile and responsive web design. While the mobile design is restrictive, responsive design is extremely flexible.

Mobile design often serves as a limited version of a website to be used on tablets and on smartphones. This means that it provides users with the bare basics that the website has to offer, and limits them from seeing and using the website to its full potential. On the other hand, responsive design makes it possible for a website to resize and reflow its layout according to the user's screen size. This means that with responsive design, a website manages to adapt to a new environment and maintain the same stunning typefaces, images, and navigational options.

3. **Website layout can retain or expel viewers**

The website layout determines the kind of experience a user will have, and will ultimately determine whether that user will have the patience to see what you have to offer, or whether to click the "back" button to search for information elsewhere. A successful website is one that has a clear and scannable layout, enabling the viewers to skim through the website and find key information quickly.

4. **Updated websites have more viewership**

An outdated website will not only fail to show up effectively in search engine results, but it will also have unexpected formatting issues that will prevent it from being properly displayed in the web browser. Therefore, a website that is outdated may not gather as many views as a constantly updated one.

Since the devices and browsers that are used to access websites are constantly changing, the manner in which those websites are developed and designed must change as well. To achieve this, a web designer must keep up with the latest coding standards, search engine algorithms and browser compatibility updates. This ensures that the websites keep up with whatever changes that are made to the devices and other software that are used to access them.

5. **Templates are restrictive**

For someone who is looking for an easy way out, use of templates is the way to go. They help anyone to create a website while concealing their cluelessness of coding knowledge. All you need to do is to choose from a wide range of pre-designed templates and voila! Even though you are presented with the option of using template-based websites, it would be much better to use a customized design.

While pre-packaged templates make the process of website creation easy and stress-free, they can be very restricting. Not only do they contain unnecessary design elements, but most of them are inflexible in what they will allow for. In order for you to maintain the credibility that you have tried so hard to build, it would be best to create a custom-made web presence that is catered to your specific needs and those of your esteemed customers.

6. **The Website's code affects search engine listings**

Even if you have the most visually-appealing website on the internet, it won't matter at all if you don't have an audience to view it. Web experts ensure that the manner in which websites are coded helps the target audience to find those websites easily once they type specific keywords into the search engines.

Search engines are a great source of new traffic to websites, which is important for you to take additional steps to optimize fully your website for those search engines. It all starts with coding best practices, as well as making sure that the foundation of your website compatible with the search engines.

7. **Videos and images have a powerful impact on websites**

Multimedia content can either have a positive or a negative impact on your website, depending on how you use it. While the use of images and videos can help to grab the attention of your audience, they can also significantly damage your websites performance. For instance, large video and image files can slow down the loading time of your site, meaning that your visitors will have to wait too long for your page to load.

To ensure that the multimedia content you use helps to engage visitors rather than drive them away, you should use videos and images that are optimized for your website. You should also avoid outdated multimedia formats (i.e. Flash) that aren't supported by a majority of today's mobile device platforms. Instead, you should opt for current standards such as HTML5 video, so that viewers can be able to access your media from a wide range of devices, including smartphones, tablets and computers.

The intricacies of web design are indeed mind-blowing, and they require a high level of updated attentiveness to detail to develop the best website possible. Keep the above facts in mind as you move forward with your website development.

CRUCIAL COMPONENTS OF ANY WEBSITE DESIGN

89% of the users search the web before making a purchase decision. This is according to the Digital Influence Index 2012. In most cases, your website is the customer's first impression of your business and its products. The outlook, content, and feel of your site are the core drivers of those first impressions.

Appealing websites are a decisive factor in engaging and retaining users online. The surprising thing is that users take milliseconds

to decide whether your site is relevant or not.

To be precise, it takes 50 to 500 milliseconds

for users to pass a decision about your site.

This is according to a study conducted by

Harvard in 2013. The study also revealed

some notable statistics:

- First impressions based on website

  design amounted to 94% (content is

  important, but it becomes ineffective

  when implanted in poor design)

- Websites that are good-looking and appealing are perceived to be trustworthy and usable.

- 75% of the users admitted to making a judgment about the credibility of the company/business based on their website design. This, however, was according to a study that was done by Stanford Web Credibility Research.

These statistics reveal that your individual, business, or company website should be relevant, appealing and optimized. Before we narrow down to how a website is set and designed, let's first focus on the major components of website design.

While every web designers may take a different route when building and designing a website, they all do have a common checklist. From visuals and space, to call-to-action and search functionality, these are the things that ought to be on a website.

1. **Space**

Space is a crucial design tool because it dictates everything- from readability to flow.

Designers are coming up with new ways of using space. Nowadays, most websites have increased the spacing between the lines of text as well as including vast spaces.

However, when modifying space, make sure to be consistent; similar elements should take up similar spacing. There should be consistency between the lines in a paragraph, as should the amount of the wrap-around images.

A spacious content will appeal more than content crammed into a smaller location on the web pages.

How do you modify space? Start with the key elements such as the navigation menus. Make sure that elements are organized in a consistent spacious manner. This will make each word or button stand out evidently on its own.

2. **About Us Page**

It's important for site owners, be it small or large business, tell users who exactly they are. The About Us page should tell the visitor what you do and who you are. It can highlight the company's goals and philosophies or the company history. The page can also be a place for success stories or users testimonials. This page can also provide a gateway to social media profiles or related pages. It should be simple, short and keyword-dense. However, the keywords should flow naturally. Use the About Us page to give your company and brand a little personality. You can also include a short

company biography and photos of your team.

3. **Simple Navigation**

Navigation needs to be kept simple and easy

to identify. It's also central to maintain the

minimum number of navigational menus in

order to avoid confusing users. Depending on

the needs of the site, five to ten navigational

menus are ideal.

Navigation also features tools that help user to

navigate through the website. Sites that have

parallax scrolling often include features like

directional arrows to make navigation simpler

and more user-friendly. Use navigation as the

basis when building a website. Remember to

keep your menus to the minimum possible.

4. **Contact Information**

Contact information should appear on the

Contact Us page, or in the header of the main

page. Either way, it can work well depending

on the design of your site and if you make it

highly visible. Include the phone number and

physical address. It can be frustrating for

users to lack your contacts when they need

you. Therefore, add your contact information to all the headers or footers.

5. **Signup or Call-to-Action**

In most cases, a business website provides a gateway to an action- be it sales, gathering contact information, or providing information. Therefore, call to action reminders needs to be strong and obvious.

You need first to determine what your site is supposed to do (the objective of your website). After that, design it in a way that the contrast, space, and color lead users to the call to action buttons. The call to action can

lead users to the company contacts or signup

form. Make the signup process/form simple

and quick to fill out. Use contrasting colors

and obvious wordings such as, Download,

Buy Now, Join, Sign up Free, etc.

6. **Search Box**

It's very frustrating to manually look for older

information or a product that you remember

seeing on a site. This is where search box

comes in. This tool is crucial, especially for a

returning user. Design and place the search

box in a way that's not obstructive but easy to use. The box should be big enough to accommodate the item names on your site. If you opt to use a search icon, just use the ordinary magnifying glass.

7. **Great images**

Visuals are eye-catching, and, therefore, you need to draw users to your site by creating stunning visuals. Great illustrations or images are an easy way to use visuals. Use few images to show the users business products, company employees, or just anything related to your site to entice users. It's much better to rely on custom images rather than the stocked images. Customized images create a unique visual experience.

8. Informational Footer

Footers provide a way in which one can share vast information to your users without interfering with the design. Because they are fixed at the bottom your webpage, it's logical to insert a small site map, contact information, and context links for your site.

Keep your footer simple and make it useful. Whether you opt for link-style or couple of buttons design, the footer should be used to mesh your website. Make it easy to use.

9. **Web Fonts**

There was a time when the web was filled with many typefaces- Courier, Arial, - because most browsers and computers could read them. That has changed, and there are no limitations nowadays. However, web fonts are still crucial for licensing and compatibility. By employing a web search font, designers don't need to maintain certain texts using images as a type is type on the web. You can start with a Google Web Fonts, which is absolutely free. Implement the set of interesting and beautiful typefaces into your website without worrying about compatibility having to spend on licensing.

10. **Style For Buttons**

Each and every button on your site should be distinguishable as a button. They should take the same design feel and effects and same shape regardless of location or purpose.

Creating a discrete set of buttons can be an overwhelming task for a site that has a handful of clickable items. In that case, consider using a design kit to come up with a consistent and distinct set of elements. Develop a unique set of buttons for your site and stick to it. Also, create a consistent color theme and a consistent shape and style of the button.

There are tons of components to effective website design, but these ten elements are the most important and common.

WEBSITE DESIGN

Web design is a broad term that incorporates developing a website and designing the web pages. You cannot separate the two as they go hand in hand. The two aspect of web design requires basic computer knowledge, access to the internet and computer, a free HTML editor and a web server. With that in place, one can now develop and design a website.

Web development is a multifaceted and complex process that has a lot of moving parts. Much like constructing a house, the

process calls for expertise and require skills

from different field brought together to

produce a website that meets the strategies,

needs, and goals of the business or

organization.

This section will cover the five major

components of a website; the constituents that

bring a website to life. They include:

1. Strategy

2. User experience

3. Design

4. Technology and

5. Marketing

A) **STRATEGY**

Before one begins to develop or design a website, they must first have a strategy. A well-crafted strategy involves defining the problem and identifying a digital approach that will be used to solve the specified problem. While different organizations have a different starting point, the approach to solving the business problem is always similar.

Sketching the blueprints of your website is much like establishing the blueprint for your house. You cannot sketch the house blueprint without knowing the number of bedrooms, closets, and bathrooms that you'll need. You'll need to know the number of people who'll live in that house.

Likewise, thoughtful research will be the footing of a user-centric web design and a crucial part when coming up with a design that supports your site's visitors. This research will help you discover and dig what's important to your users and business.

To identify a strategy or the problem to be solved by your website, you need to undertake the discovery process and have a different personal team.

The Discovery Process

A well-thought out discovery involves examining your organization/business, your audiences, your search engine optimization chances, your competitors and many other factors that are relevant to your business. During this stage, you'll be required to collect views from the key stakeholders of your business. The input gathered will help shed some light on the unique challenges and perspectives.

Stakeholders also include your current customers as well as potential customers visiting your website. The goals and expectations that the users who will be visiting your site hope to achieve are the core blocks of your website design and structure.

The Building Team

To ensure that the discovery stage is successful, you'll need to gather personas that will define each target audience needs, tasks, and goals. To guide the personas, you'll need to compile a list of the professional, technical and personal questions of who your ideal website user is. These will act as the goals for measuring the success. The questions will act as the Key Performance Indicators (KPIs). These KPIs will help direct the entire scope of the website and act as your strategy control guide.

Some of the questions you can ask during the Building Team development include:

1. What's the age of your target audience

2. What is there reason(s) for visiting your website

3. What are their proficient backgrounds

4. What devices do they normally use to access your site (e.g., desktop, tablets, mobile, etc.)

Having established the website strategy, you can now focus on the user needs.

B) **USER EXPERIENCE**

Once you identify the requirements and need of the house residents, one can now start to conceptualize how the house will adapt to their needs. This is similar for the user Experience process (UX process) of a website.

The user experience centers aims to meet the exact needs of the targeted users by creating a pleasing and memorable interactive experience. To achieve this, you have to convert your strategic goals into meaningful interactions and executable tactics that will create a pleasing digital experience and give your uses what they intended to get from your site; content.

Content

Under the user experience, the main thing that most users are interested in is content. With that in mind, you need to understand who needs your content, where they search for it, and what their thoughts about it are. After that, you'll need to know the structure that your content will take. This includes the headlines, labels, wording and paragraph. This is called the tone. This will now help move the process from theory to the practice level. For you to succeed, your UX team needs to communicate the design decision in form of taxonomy and provide a sitemap that will act as the high-level vision of the website organization.

When developing your sitemap, consider the following;

- Labels. What positions should the labels take and will the users understand the navigation labels?

- Information Hierarchy. Define whether your content is of primary or tertiary importance?

- Use cases. Who are your users and how will they undertake a specific task?

Once the labels, hierarchy, taxonomy and use cases are well-understood, the UX team will then blend these elements into wireframes. The wireframes are the website strategy in absence of visuals and are commonly called the website blueprints.

Wireframes can be of different levels including:

- Low Fidelity. These are the Hand-drawn or digital wireframes which comprises of labels on a plain background.

- Paper- These are hand-drawn wireframes

- High-Fidelity- These are the wireframes that convey your site color schemes, logos, and other basic graphics.

- Clickable prototypes. These are semi-functional layouts that offer a high preview level of the definite site by allowing users to click around.

Testing Usability

Now that the wireframe has been developed, you need to test it to ensure the success of your site. Select a sample of users who will act as a representative of the main audience of your website and allow them to view and work with the wireframes. To authenticate the wireframes, the subjects in tests will complete the tasks that your website is designed to carry out.

What to observe during the user testing session?

- Was it easily navigable?

- Did the user accomplish their intended task easily?

- Were the calls to action rightly placed?

- Was the information misplaced or hard to find?

- Did the user understand the labels and content?

The answers to the above question will help you in refining and revising the system as you proceed to the visual design stage.

c) **DESIGN**

The design stage is where you'll finally see your project materializing. Just like building a model of your house, the design stage puts the UX concepts into a tangible composition that your audience can relate.

Elements in the Design Phase

Mood Boards

Just like the way an interior designer starts by redesigning a living room, the very first step to designing the website is to create a mood

board. A mood board is the appealing blend of

your brand colors, logos, photography, icons

and fonts all in single document.

The mood board gives you foreshadow of the

visuals arrangements on your site rather than

the web merchant revealing one huge

deliverable at the end of the website

development process.

A Mood board enables you to get an overall

feel and look of your site before the user

meanders down the wrong path. Once the

mood board is finalized, you can then start

designing the homepage and any other

webpage of your site (How to develop and

design webpage is in the next chapter).

Responsive Design

Having approved the visuals in your site, you'll

then consult the front-end website developer

to discuss about the responsive web design

layouts (RWD layouts). Responsive web

design is developing and designing a site with

flexible design layouts that respond to the

device which the user is using to visit your site, hence the name responsive.

Your website designer will design your site using a layout that is appropriate for various devices. The UX team will have to test the site at this point using different devices to get a feel of the experience.

D) TECHNOLOGY

Whether you intend to set up a ten pages or thousand pages website, selecting an appropriate content management system (CMS) is crucial to ensuring the success of your site. The content management system acts as the footing of your site. Using our usual metaphor of building a house, the CMS is comparable to the electricity, plumbing, air conditioner, and insulation and heating.

For your site, a CMS will provide you with

simple tools for creating, modifying and

publishing your content. It will also help you in

sales support and marketing including

analytics, campaign development, workflows,

and customer relationship managements

(CRM) integrations.

How to Choose an Appropriate CMS

When evaluating the type of CMS that suits

your website needs, there are many factors

that will need to be taken into consideration as

each CMS has its pros and drawbacks. Some

help you to work at ease while others are exceedingly customizable. By choosing the right content management system, you'll have prevented unwanted issues and drawbacks and you'll help the organization to concentrate on delivering significant results from your site.

Before choosing the CMS for your site, ask yourself the following questions?

- Do you need advanced marketing capabilities such as email integration, campaign creation and A/B testing?

- Do you require authorization to the secure content?

- Will you need a tech-savvy to maintain your site?

- How much traffic do you expect to your site on monthly basis?

Having answered these questions, you can now evaluate the handy CMS that are available to determine the one that will support your needs.

Integration

Integrating your site with internal systems or third-part vendors is a phase that needs a lot of consideration and should be evaluated carefully. Different integrations present different complexities regardless of whether you are capturing a user's order details or integrating a CRM.

Spend significant time at the start of the project to determine the involvedness of the integration needs and the steps to take to properly integrate your site with the internal system or third-party application program

interface (API).

Hosting

A good and reliable hosting plan is arguably

the backbone and the engine of your website

project. After all, your new, pleasing and

attractive website is inaccessible without

hosting.

Infrastructural needs of your site should be

taken into consideration from the time of

planning the project, through its launch, and even when it's running.

The three classifications of hosting solutions include;

- Cloud hosting in shared environment

- Cloud hosting in dedicated environment

- Owner disposition of hosting servers

Each of the above listed hosting solutions poses different challenges and therefore, you need to take some time to consider which is ideal for your website. Hosting is a core consideration that should be taken seriously.

Choosing the right host and maintain your

website are two factors that will guarantee

reliability and success of your organization.

E) **MARKETING**

It is said that no one shows up for a private wedding party if they never got an invitation in the first place. Similarly, all the design, UX, and technology in the website world won't function if you cannot drive and maintain traffic to your site. Depending on the business goals and needs, different marketing strategies should be taken into account to best compliment the overall business strategy. While you can use a myriad of platform to market your website, let's focus on the Search

Engine Marketing duo; paid search and

Search Engine Optimization

Search Engine Optimization

Many people are deceived by the false belief

that optimizing your site is easy. It demands a

lot of time, effort, and money to do well and to

do right. True SEO creativity requires

analytical and scientific mindset as well as an

artful eye and talent.

How does the SEO WORK?

The internet user is the author of SEO. The users turn to search engines such as Google and Bing to access information about everything they need. The search engines return the results based on several factors-many of which are unknown to many but the search engines themselves. Some of these factors include accuracy, Keywords and the relevancy of results.

To make sure that your site is fully optimized, you need the help of the SEO expert so that they can take all these factors into consideration and come up with a strategy that will make your website rank higher in Google search result page. The SEO expert will also determine the keywords that matter most to your targeted audience. No gimmick or tricks. Just sheer hard work, user-centric approach, and a lot of analysis.

An SEO expert will make recommendations based on the following:

- Title tags

- Content

- H1s and H2s

- Meta descriptions

- XML sitemaps

- URLs

Paid Search

Paid search, commonly referred to as PPC or pay-per-click, is a more effective approach to search engine marketing, especially when compared to SEO. Paid search is an advertising strategy in which one get paid for placing ads on search engines.

All the paid search ad avenues such as Google AdWords, allow one to buy ads that compliment your site keywords or the keywords that you want to appear on your site. Unlike in SEO where the ranking of the website's keywords occurs naturally over time, paid search give you a chance to rank for competitive keywords at a significant price.

The Bidding Wars

The paid search uses a bidding system when placing ads. The website owner tells Google the amount they're willing to spend on a keyword and Google display the keyword to the users based on the existing price of the keyword. If your bid is not high enough, the number of ad's placement will reduce or fail to be shown at all. Therefore, the more competitive your keyword is, the more other websites will be willing to spend on it.

Marketing your site using SEO and Paid Search are continuous processes that demand constant strategizing, monitoring, and analyzing.

FACTORS THAT AFFECT THE COST OF WEB DESIGN

Whether you intend to establish a new website, or you are thinking of redesigning an existing site, there are cost implications that you must be prepared to face. The following are the major factors that usually affect the cost of web design:

Complexity of the Website

The more complex a website is to design, the more time it will be required to build it. If you involve a professional web designer, you will be charged on an hourly basis. Simple designs or template-based designs may take a short time to complete, but more complexes or custom-made design might take longer. Therefore, the more time the designer will require designing your website, the more money you will end up paying.

Availability of a Content List

Do you have a list of all the functional features and pages for your website? If you already have a content list beforehand, then the creation of your website design can start right away. If you will be relying on the web designer to come up with the list, then the cost will vary depending on the amount of research to be done. For example, the designer might charge a fee for analyzing your web traffic statistics and interviewing your target audience. The more involved the web designer will be, the higher the cost of designing your website.

Amount of Content Needed

Do you have content that needs to be rewritten for your new site or do you need new content to be written? It will be cost effective to write your content, but if you intend to hire a web content writer, then you will incur a cost. The cost for content creation will depend on the amount of research needed, as well as the total number of pages to be written.

Content Management System (CMS)

A CMS makes it possible for you to make changes to your website's pages, photos, and text in just a few clicks. Popular content management system platforms are usually free, with the web designer's cost coming from design customization and configuration. The costs for an open source content management system vary depending on the complexity of the design and the number of pages on the website.

Design's Responsiveness to Mobile Devices

In this digital era when many people access the internet via their mobile devices, it is crucial that the website design be made responsive. Therefore, if you intend to design a website with responsive design, you will need to pay a little extra.

EFFECTIVE WEB DESIGN PRACTICES YOU MUST ADHERE TO

Some people don't know how crucial the design of their websites is for conversion until they come up with something that looks like crap and ends up losing the very same credibility they had hoped to build. Web design is not just something that web designers do – it is a form of marketing. The design of your website is your product, and the more you let other people learn about it,

the better results you will get. The following
are the top 4 effective web design principles
that you must follow:

1. **Using prominent visuals**

If you would like to grab the attention of your
website visitors, then it's best to use
prominent visuals. Visual hierarchy is basically
the order in which the eye perceives what it
sees. Some parts of your websites are more
important than others, such as value
propositions, forms, and calls to action.
Therefore, you must implement the principle

of visual hierarchy by making those parts more visible than others to ensure that visitors will not miss them.

There are various ways in which you can implement visual hierarchy, i.e. you can make those important parts more prominent by enlarging the text size, or by using a different color. You should also rank elements accordingly and in positions that are easy for the visitor to find. This way, the visitors will be in a position to find whatever it is they want easily.

2. **Effective wording**

The ability to use words properly and effectively is probably the most important skill that a web designer should possess. A good web designer is the one that is sufficiently skilled with writing and editing copy, and can be able to turn a website into a great success even if it is graphically plain.

Effective wording involves crafting a number of web pages that communicate, inform and call site visitors to take the desired actions. Besides being a key for brand communication, effective wording is also vital for usability. Proper use of words is more efficient than icons and other images. It is with words that you can also optimize your website for search engines and make it easy for the targeted audience to find your website. The better your writing, the better your website will perform.

3. **Narrowing down choices**

This helps greatly when it comes to decision making. The Hick's law stipulates that the time required to make a decision increases with every additional choice. This is akin to the

Paradox of Choice that says that the more choice is given to you the easier it is for you to choose nothing. Back to web design, the more options you give your website viewers, the more difficult it will be for them to use your site.

In order for you to provide your website viewers with a more interactive and enjoyable experience, you should eliminate choices by getting rid of distracting options during the design process. If you are having a wide range of products on offer, it's best to add filters to help your customers in decision making.

4. **Incorporating multimedia content**

Doing so makes a website interesting and engaging. It is a good idea to not only use text but to also incorporate images and videos to your website design. It is much easier to communicate your ideas with visual content than with text. Nevertheless, inappropriate use of multimedia content may harm your website's performance, thus drive the target audience away. Like earlier mentioned, large image and video files may take long to load and viewers may get impatient and decide to try out another website. It is, therefore, important that you incorporate multimedia tactfully to avoid this.

5. **Maintaining Simplicity**

Simplicity has always been an important element of web design, and it will surely continue to remain so. It's important that communicate your objectives in a simple, clear and concise manner so that the site viewers can fathom what you are trying to communicate at the first glance. As much as you would like to create an impression of sophistication and professionalism, it's imperative that you keep things simple. Too many buttons and features can only lead to one thing – too much confusion. Most viewers appreciate a website designs that don't require a lot of brainpower to fathom what's being communicated.

6. **Avoid overstuffing**

One of the big mistakes you can do when creating a website is to overstuff your web pages. The last thing you want is for your site visitors to be reminded of a local state fair that's full of brilliant lights and neon signs whenever they see your website. An overcrowded website is more like a state fair in the sense that it has got everything fighting for your attention, making it hard for you to figure out what your next move should be. What you want is a website design that doesn't confuse the viewers and directs them to exactly where they should click.

7. **Make use of your Own Photos. Don't Photoshop!**

As earlier mentioned, integrating multimedia content with text content is a wise thing to do when creating a website. While there are so many cool photos online, it would be a huge mistake if you took other people's photos and used them as your own. Plagiarism is one of the biggest crimes you can commit when creating content, and posting photos that aren't yours isn't a less crime either. To be on the safe side, make use of your own photos.

8. Avoid Jargon and Business Speak

No matter your target audience, it will be more helpful to use a language that is easy to understand. This means that you should come up with web-friendly text that does not call for a dictionary to be comprehended. You should write short sentences, make use of bullet points and subheads where necessary, and avoid using heavy vocabulary that can get your readers lost somewhere along the way.

9. Ensure that your website is easy to navigate

It's very easy to lose your patience online, especially when the website you are trying to view is hard to navigate through. To ensure that your visitors are not aggravated, it is imperative that you make your website design in such a way that allows visitors to find all the information they need in a seamless manner. This means that you should provide all the relevant links and put them conveniently so that they can be easily seen and accessed.

10. **Adopt responsive design**

Responsive design is a crucial element due to the fact that most people are accessing the internet from a wide range of mobile devices, including smartphones, tablets, and laptops. If the majority of your target audience is not able to access your website through their mobile devices, then they will not hesitate to look what your competition has to offer. Therefore, it is crucial that you adopt a responsive design that allows users to access your website seamlessly regardless of the devices they use.

11. Instant Access

This is another vital element to consider when coming up with a web design. Measures have to be put in place to ensure that site visitors will have easy and instant access to the website whenever they visit. This involves keeping the landing page simple and ensuring that visitors are instantly directed to the information they need without delays. It's also important that crucial information such as the email address, physical address, and phone number is provided on the first page.

12. Use compelling content

To make your website and business look approachable to your target audience, it would be wise to incorporate some appealing and compelling content to your website design. Such content will not only attract new viewers to your website, but it will ensure that those viewers will keep coming back to your website for more.

13. Integrate Social Media Sites

In this day and age, the power of social media cannot be underestimated. To many, social media is probably the most powerful marketing tool that you can use today. It is, therefore, highly recommended that you make your web design in such a way that allows an integration of several social media sites such as LinkedIn, Twitter, Facebook, etc. For example, you can put several social media links or buttons on your websites that when clicked will connect your viewers to your social media pages for further engagements and interactions.

14. **Look at your competitors' websites**

You can never know how good (or bad) your website design is until you look at your competitors' websites. Even before you create your own website, it is advisable that you take some time to see what your competitors have to offer, and see which designs are more compelling to the target audience. This will give one an idea of which designs will be more appropriate for your audience.

15. Involve a professional web designer

If you do not have what it takes to create a competitive website, it would be prudent on your part to involve a professional web designer to do the job for you. You need an expert with the relevant skills to develop a website that communicates your objectives in a manner that your target audience will find professional and at the same time, easy to understand.

Those are the top 15 best practices for creating a website design. You have to keep in mind that having a carefully crafted website design will not only be a part of your online marketing plan but will also be the

cornerstone of your overall marketing strategy.

FACTORS TO CONSIDER BEFORE DECIDING WHETHER TO BUILD A DIY WEBSITE OR HIRE A WEB DESIGN SERVICE

One of the considerations that you will have to make once you decide to have your own website is whether to do it yourself or to hire a web designer. Well, while you might find it more economical to develop your own site without professional help, there are some aspects that must be looked into first. They

include:

Your specific needs

The good thing about designing your own

website is that you are familiar with every

single detail that fits your image, products or

services. This means that you might be in a

good position to create a website that gives

the best and realistic reflection of your

business to your target audience. If you are

competent enough to come up with a

purposeful website that appeals to your

specific target audience, then you can go ahead and develop the website. If not, it is best to hire a professional designer to do the work for you.

Your budget

The costs that are involved in hiring a professional are certainly higher compared to the amount you would spend while designing a website by yourself. If you are operating on a tight budget, then it can be economical to design your website. However, if you are designing a website for a large company that has enough money to spend, it is more ideal to involve an expert in designing the website.

Urgency of the website to go live

If you are creating your personal website that doesn't need to go live within the shortest time possible, then you can take all the time you need to design it all by yourself. However, if there is great need for the website to be functional immediately, then the best thing to do is to hire a professional. An expert has all the skills and experience needed to develop and design an appealing and functional website from scratch to completion in good time.

If there are competitors in play

If you intend to design a website that provides information about products or services that are highly advertised online, it is best that you let a professional design you a competitive site. An experienced web designer knows what it takes to attract the kind of audience you are striving to attract, thus can create a website that will help you achieve just that. With billions of websites on the internet today, what do you do to make your website stand out from all the rest? Well, a professional web designer is best placed to create a unique website that will keep you on a competitive edge.

If an image of professionalism is required

If your aim is to have a website that looks and feels professional, then hiring a professional web designer might be a good option. It is very easy to distinguish between a professional and a homemade website. If you would like your website to convey a sense of security to your customers, it is important that

you hire a professional web designer.

Usability in Web Design – Understanding

Web Users

"In 2016, usability testing, not visual design, is determining the failure or success of a website."

In this chapter, we will cover the main heuristics, principles and methods for responsive web design – methods which, followed properly, can positively impact the user's perception of the presented information and lead to sophisticated web design. I normally tell my web design students that for them to design effective websites, they must first understand how web users think, how they interact with online content, and their browsing behaviors. In the following chapter, we will cover all these elements.

1. How Users Think

On a general note, users' behavior on the internet is not very different from their behavior in brick and motor stores. They glance through each new page, skim through a little of the text, and open the first link that grabs their attention or closely resemble the information, product, or the services they are searching for. As soon as the search result page appears, they look for something clickable or useful and click. However, if the link takes them to a page that does not offer them the information or the product they are looking for, they immediately click the back arrow and on to competitors site.

In Short, to Drive Conversion, a Website Must Make a Great First Impression

The website represents what the business is and what it offers. When visitors land on it for the first time, they seek to know;

- Is it trustworthy?

- Is the site credible?

- Does it look professional?

- Can this site give me what I am looking for?

- Am I in the right place

- Does the website make me feel welcome?

Note the following;

- If a webpage gives users high quality content, they will be ready to compromise a poor web design and advertisements and stay on the page. This is the primary reason some poorly designed sites with great content continues to get huge traffic over the years. The point is, "The quality of webpage is more important than the page design which complements it."

- Web users insist on immediate gratification, they're impatient. If a site does not meet their expectations, the designer failed to get the job done and the enterprise will lose money. The more the cognitive load and irresponsive the navigation is, the more the users will abandon the website and visit alternative sites.

- Web users follow their intuition. In many cases, they muddle through as opposed to reading the information the designer has offered.

- Users want to be in control. They want to be able to control the browsing and get consistent data presentation throughout the website. That is they do not want any window popping up and

they want the freedom to get back with

the back arrow to the website they were

on. As such, it's always a good practice

to avoid opening links in new browser

windows.

And a no-brainer;

Make sure visitors can properly view the site

regardless of the browser they are no, or the

application they are browsing from.

2. Do Not Make Users Think

As Krug's first law of Usability outlines, "Webpages should be obvious and self-explanatory. When designing a site, you must make the architecture and navigation as intuitive as possible. Ideally, make use of moderate visual clues, a clear structure, and recognizable links.

A recent HubSpot study tells that 75% of web users say that most important factor on a site is the ease of finding information. If users cannot see what they are looking for, they will quickly leave and visitor competitors' sites.

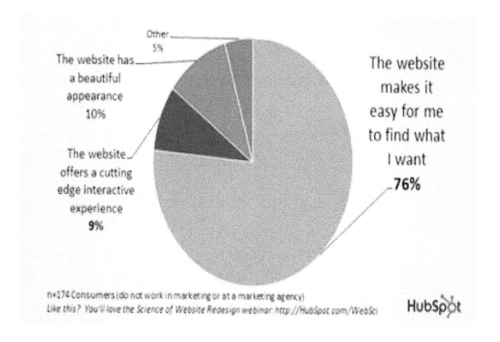

Other 5%

The website has a beautiful appearance 10%

The website offers a cutting edge interactive experience 9%

The website makes it easy for me to find what I want 76%

n=174 Consumers (do not work in marketing or at a marketing agency)
Like this? You'll love the Science of Website Redesign webinar: http://HubSpot.com/WebSci

HubSpot

Vital Features in Website Navigation

- Keep the primary navigation simple, and at the top of the site.

- Add navigate in the site footer.

- Add breadcrumbs on all pages except the homepage so that visitors are aware of the navigation trail.

- Add a search box towards the top of the site so that visitors can easily navigate your site by keywords.

- Do not offer "Too Many" navigation options on a single page.

- Do not go too deep, its best practice to maintain your navigation at no more than 3 levels.

- Avoid complicated JavaScript such as Flash in your navigation. Most mobile phones cannot play Flash; thus, they won't be able to navigate your site. The same case applies to browsers without an up-to-date version of Flash Player installed.

- In short, make the navigation simple; do not make your visitors think where they should go to get what they want. Ideally, put yourself in the shoes of the visitor, and ask yourself whether it's obvious on the site where one should go to find

what he or she wants.

3. Do Not Squanders Web Users' Patience

In all projects where the client wants you to

direct visitors to a tool or some services, keep

the users' requirement minimal. The less the

work required for a user's to actually test a

service or product, the more likely that a new

lead will actually test it. Visitors are ready to

see what you are offering, but they are not

going to be patient enough to fill pages of web

forms.

Allow your users to explore the website and

discover your services without asking for

personal data. It's unreasonable to force users

to give their email to access a certain feature.

The developer of 37Singals team, Ryan

Singer, says, "Web users will most likely

provide their emails after they have seen your

services work; it gives them an idea of what

you will be giving them in return"

sign up for stikkit

email address

editor@smashingmagazine.com

nickname

smashing

password

•••••••••

password again

•••••••••••

☑ I agree to the Stikkit **Terms of Use** and **Privacy Policy**. (We also provide a **summary of your rights and obligations**.)

sign up

This web form from <u>Stikkit</u> is a great example

of a user friendly web form. It requires very

little input from the users and that is

comforting. Exactly what good design should

aim to deliver.

Clearly, Mite collects more information from visitors. But note that their registration can be accomplished in less than 40 seconds – since the webpage is horizontally oriented, users do not even need to scroll the webpage.

I normally advise designers to remove all barriers; do not require users to register before seeing what you are offering first. A forced registration is a huge impediment on navigation and can easily divert incoming traffic.

www.ingramcontent.com/pod-product-compliance
Lightning Source LLC
Chambersburg PA
CBHW071222050326

40689CB00011B/2416